NEW YORK TEST PREP
Reading and Writing
Common Core Workbook
Grade 4

© 2014 by Test Master Press New York

All rights reserved. No part of this book may be reproduced or transmitted in any form or by any means, electronic, mechanical, photocopying, recording, or otherwise without prior written permission.

ISBN 978-1505831160

Reading and Writing, Common Core Workbook, Grade 4

CONTENTS

Introduction	4
Reading and Writing Practice Set 1	5
Short Passages, Long Passage with Essay, Personal Narrative Writing Task	
Reading and Writing Practice Set 2	17
Short Passages, Short Story Writing Task, Opinion Piece Writing Task	
Reading and Writing Practice Set 3	27
Short Passages, Long Passage with Essay, Personal Narrative Writing Task	
Reading and Writing Practice Set 4	41
Short Passages, Opinion Piece Writing Task, Short Story Writing Task	
Reading and Writing Practice Set 5	51
Short Passages, Long Passage with Essay, Personal Narrative Writing Task	
Reading and Writing Practice Set 6	65
Short Passages, Short Story Writing Task, Opinion Piece Writing Task	
Reading and Writing Practice Set 7	75
Short Passages, Long Passage with Essay, Explanatory Writing Task	
Reading and Writing Practice Set 8	87
Short Passages, Opinion Piece Writing Task, Short Story Writing Task	
Reading and Writing Practice Set 9	99
Short Passages, Long Passage with Essay, Explanatory Writing Task	
Reading and Writing Practice Set 10	111
Short Passages, Short Story Writing Task, Opinion Piece Writing Task	
Answer Key	123
Informational/Explanatory Writing Rubric	134
Opinion Writing Rubric	135
Narrative Writing Rubric	136

Reading and Writing, Common Core Workbook, Grade 4

INTRODUCTION
For Parents, Teachers, and Tutors

Developing Common Core Reading and Writing Skills

The state of New York has adopted the Common Core Learning Standards. These standards describe what students are expected to know. Students will be instructed based on these standards and the New York Common Core English Language Arts Test will include questions based on these standards. This workbook will develop the Common Core reading and writing skills that students are expected to have, while preparing students for the state tests and giving students practice completing a range of reading and writing tasks. The emphasis in this workbook is on writing skills, but complementary reading skills are also covered as students complete tasks involving providing written answers to reading comprehension questions.

Completing Practice Sets

This workbook is divided into 10 practice sets. Each practice set includes four tasks that progress from simple to more complex. The types of tasks are described below.

Task Type	Details
Short Passage with Questions	These tasks contain a short passage followed by reading comprehension questions requiring written answers. They also include a Core Writing Skills Practice exercise that focuses on one key writing skill. These exercises may require students to respond to a text, complete a research project, or complete a writing task.
Long Passage with Essay Question	These tasks contain a long passage followed by an essay question requiring a written answer of 1 to 2 pages. They also include hints and planning guidance to help students develop effective writing skills.
Personal Narrative Writing Task	These tasks contain a writing prompt for a personal narrative, as well as hints and planning guidance.
Short Story Writing Task	These tasks contain a writing prompt for a story, as well as hints and planning guidance.
Opinion Piece Writing Task	These tasks contain a writing prompt for an opinion piece, as well as hints and planning guidance.
Explanatory Writing Task	These tasks contain a writing prompt for an essay, as well as hints and planning guidance.

By completing the practice sets, students will have experience with all types of Common Core writing tasks. This includes writing in response to passages, writing all the types of texts covered in the Common Core standards, gathering information from sources, and completing research projects.

Some of the writing tasks also include guides for editing and revising completed work. This encourages students to review their work and improve on it, while the checklists help students focus on the key criteria that work is judged on. This will prepare students for the writing tasks found on assessments, as well as guide students on the key features of strong writing.

Preparing for the New York Common Core English Language Arts Test

The New York Common Core English Language Arts Test assesses reading, writing, and language skills. The test includes short-response questions where students write an answer of a few sentences as well as extended-response questions where students write an essay based on a text. The tests are also more rigorous than past tests, focus more strongly on analyzing text closely and using evidence from text, require students to complete more complex tasks, and have a stronger emphasis on higher-order thinking skills like analyzing, evaluating, or making connections.

This workbook will help prepare students for the tests. The questions and exercises will develop the more advanced Common Core skills, give students ongoing practice with more rigorous questions, provide extensive experience providing written answers to short-response and extended-response questions, help students write effective essays, and develop higher-order thinking skills. This will ensure that students have the skills and experience they need to perform well on the state tests.

Reading and Writing

Practice Set 1

This practice set contains four writing tasks. These are described below.

Task 1: Short Passage with Questions

This task has a short passage followed by questions. Read each question carefully. Then write your answer in the space provided.

You can also practice writing skills by completing the Core Writing Skills Practice exercise.

Task 2: Short Passage with Questions

This task has a short passage followed by questions. Read each question carefully. Then write your answer in the space provided.

You can also practice writing skills by completing the Core Writing Skills Practice exercise.

Task 3: Long Passage with Essay Question

This task has a longer passage with an essay question. Read the passage, complete the planning page, and then write or type your answer.

Task 4: Personal Narrative Writing Task

This final task requires you to write a personal narrative. Read the writing prompt, complete the planning page, and then write or type your answer.

Task 1: Short Passage with Questions

Mystery Dish

"I'm as hungry as a bear in winter," Angelo whined to his big sister Rita.

"It's time for lunch then!" Rita replied as she rummaged around in the refrigerator.

Rita found a full bowl of something and put it on the bench. Angelo took one look at it and shook his head firmly.

"Yuck! I'm not eating that!" Angelo said. "I don't even know what it is."

"Maybe we should find out what it is," Rita suggested as she grabbed a fork. She scooped a little bit of the food into her mouth. "Mmm, it's ham soup," she exclaimed as she put the bowl into the microwave.

"I love ham soup," Angelo said, as he smiled and ran to the table. "Hurry up! I'm starving and it smells amazing."

CORE WRITING SKILLS PRACTICE

What message does the passage have about being afraid of the unknown?

_____

_____

_____

_____

_____

1   What will most likely happen next in the passage?

Hint   This question is asking you to make a prediction. Use the details given to guess what will happen next.

_____

_____

_____

_____

_____

2   Identify the simile used in the passage and explain the meaning of the simile.

Hint   A simile compares two things using the words *like* or *as*.

_____

_____

_____

_____

_____

Task 2: Short Passage with Questions

The Amazing Amazon

The Amazon River in South America is the second longest river in the world. The Nile River in Africa is the longest river in the world. Different countries in South America call the river by different names. In Peru, it is called Apurimac, and in Brazil, it is the Solimoes.

Rivers of the World

River	Length (in miles)
Nile	4,100
Amazon	4,000
Yangtze	3,900
Mississippi	3,900
Yenisei	3,400

The Amazon River has a massive basin of about 3 million square miles. It is located deep in the rainforests of South America. One of the most interesting things about the river is that there is no point at which the river has a bridge across it. This is because the river flows mainly through deep rainforests, and there are few towns on the river.

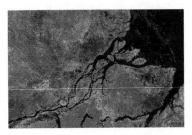

This satellite picture shows the mouth of the Amazon River. The Amazon River empties into the Atlantic Ocean on the east coast of South America.

CORE WRITING SKILLS PRACTICE
WRITE A RESEARCH REPORT

This passage gives facts and details about the Amazon River. Choose one of the American rivers listed below. Write a report giving facts and interesting details about the river.

Colorado River   Mississippi River   Missouri River

Yukon River   Yellowstone River   Rio Grande

1. The chart summarizes facts given about the Amazon River. Complete the chart using details from the passage.

The Amazon River

Location	
Length	
Basin	3 million square miles

2. Which details from the passage did you find most interesting?

Hint: This question is asking for your personal opinion. As well as describing what you found most interesting, make sure you also briefly explain why.

_____
_____
_____
_____
_____

Task 3: Long Passage with Essay Question

Directions: Read the passage below. Then answer the question that follows. Use the planning page to plan your writing. Then write or type your essay.

How to Revise

When you revise, you go over what you have learned. Revising is an important process. It helps you learn, remember, and apply what you know. It is also a good idea to revise before quizzes and exams. This will help keep material fresh in your mind. Here are some tips on how to revise well.

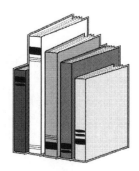

Find Your Place

To revise for an exam, you must first find a quiet and relaxing environment. Somewhere you feel most comfortable works best. It should be in a place where you will not be disturbed or distracted.

Get Set Up

Gather your books and keep them neatly organized along with your papers and stationary. It is also wise to have a fully working Internet connection handy. This helps you to access information that will help you with your studies. You can then start revising by reading your textbooks and making notes to help you learn.

Take Your Time

It's a good idea to make revising part of your weekly routine. The best way to do this is to study every school day. You should set a time each day that you study. You should take care to make sure that you do not revise for too long. Study for a set amount of time so that you can maintain your concentration. Make sure you study for no more than 2 hours at a time, and that you take regular breaks every half hour or so. This will keep you fresh and able to take in information.

Stay Organized

It can be very helpful to set up a system so you are organized. If you are taking notes, file them by subject, topic, and date. That way when you have a quiz or exam, you can easily find the right notes to study to help you prepare.

Check Your Progress

At the end of every revision session, review your notes carefully so that you can be sure that you have understood what you have learned. You may also consider writing out revision cards. You can then use these as a summary of the subjects that you have studied.

1   The author of the passage gives a lot of advice about how to revise well. Which pieces of advice did you find most helpful?

In your answer, be sure to
- describe which pieces of advice you found most helpful
- explain why you found those pieces of advice helpful
- use details from the passage in your answer
- write an answer of between 1 and 2 pages

Hint

The passage gives advice on how to revise. To answer this question, you should think about how you would apply the information. Think about which pieces of advice would most help you revise well. When you write your answer, explain how you would use the advice and how it would help you.

Planning Page

Summary
Write a brief summary of what you are going to write about.

Supporting Details
Write down the facts, details, or examples you are going to include in your answer.

Outline
Write a plan for what you are going to write. Include the main points you want to cover and the order you will cover them.

Task 4: Personal Narrative Writing Task

Directions: Read the writing prompt below. Use the planning page to plan your writing. Then write or type your answer.

Sometimes people can surprise you. They may be kinder or cleverer than you expected, or they may act in a way that surprises you.

Write a composition describing a time when someone surprised you. Explain who the person was, what they did, and why it surprised you.

Hint

Make sure you answer each part of the question. Remember that you need to include the following:
- who surprised you
- what the person did to surprise you
- why what the person did surprised you

When you write your outline, make sure that it covers all of the parts of the question.

Planning Page

Summary

Write a brief summary of what you are going to write about.

Outline

Write a plan for what you are going to write. Include the main points you want to cover and the order you will cover them.

Writing and Editing Checklist

After you finish writing your personal narrative, you can use this guide to review and edit your work. Use the questions as a guide to finding ways you can improve your work.

Writing Checklist

- ✓ Does your work have a strong opening? Does it introduce the main ideas or set the scene well?
- ✓ Is your work well-organized? Is related information grouped together? Does each paragraph have one main idea?
- ✓ Does your work have an effective ending? Does it tie up the events well?
- ✓ Is your work focused? Are there any details that do not fit with your main ideas?
- ✓ Do your ideas flow well? Have you used words and phrases to link ideas well?
- ✓ Have you used strong words? Are there words that could be replaced with better ones?
- ✓ Have you used effective descriptions? Could your descriptions be improved?
- ✓ Have you used sensory details? Could you add more sensory details to help readers imagine the scene?

Editing Checklist

- ✓ Have you used a variety of sentence structures? Are your sentences all written correctly?
- ✓ Is the grammar correct?
- ✓ Are all words spelled correctly? You can check the spelling of any words you are not sure of.
- ✓ Is punctuation used correctly?
- ✓ If dialogue is used, is it punctuated correctly?
- ✓ Are all words capitalized correctly?

Reading and Writing

Practice Set 2

This practice set contains four writing tasks. These are described below.

Task 1: Short Passage with Questions

This task has a short passage followed by questions. Read each question carefully. Then write your answer in the space provided.

You can also practice writing skills by completing the Core Writing Skills Practice exercise.

Task 2: Short Passage with Questions

This task has a short passage followed by questions. Read each question carefully. Then write your answer in the space provided.

You can also practice writing skills by completing the Core Writing Skills Practice exercise.

Task 3: Short Story Writing Task

This task requires you to write a short story. Read the writing prompt, complete the planning page, and then write or type your answer.

Task 4: Opinion Piece Writing Task

This final task requires you to write an opinion piece. Read the writing prompt, complete the planning page, and then write or type your answer.

Task 1: Short Passage with Questions

The City of Troy

The city of Troy was located in modern day Asia 5000 years ago. It was located where the country of Turkey is today. Troy is well known as the city in the "Trojan Horse" fable.

Mythology tells of Greek warriors hiding inside a gigantic wooden horse that was given to Troy as a gift. The Greek warriors in the horse were taken inside Troy's city walls. They waited until nightfall before leaving the horse. The Greek warriors were then able to open Troy's city gates from within and launch an attack. This sneaky tactic allowed the Greeks to win the war against the Trojans. Today, the term "Trojan Horse" is used to refer to any strategy that tricks an enemy into allowing the foe into their space.

CORE WRITING SKILLS PRACTICE

You can often tell what words mean by how they are used in a passage. Locate the words below in the passage. Write a definition for each word.

warriors _____

_____

tactic _____

_____

foe _____

_____

1   Explain why the Greek warriors hid inside the wooden horse.

    _____

    _____

    _____

    _____

    _____

2   The Greek warriors' plan could be described as clever or silly. Circle the word you think best describes the plan. Then explain why you chose that word.

    clever   silly

    _____

    _____

    _____

    _____

    _____

Task 2: Short Passage with Questions

Spiders

Hello! I'm a spider, hanging here,
I've been spinning my web all day.
I've been working so hard on my web,
I don't even have time to play.

Some people say that I'm scary,
It makes my feelings kind of sore.
What they really need to know,
Is that *they* scare me even more!

CORE SKILLS PRACTICE

Irony occurs when something happens that is very different from what is expected. Describe how the spider's feelings about people are ironic.

_____

_____

_____

_____

_____

_____

_____

1. The speaker in the poem is a spider. How does the spider show that it works very hard?

   Hint: Focus on what the spider says to support the idea that it works very hard.

   _____
   _____
   _____
   _____
   _____

2. Describe the rhyme pattern in the poem.

   _____
   _____
   _____
   _____
   _____

Task 3: Short Story Writing Task

Directions: Read the writing prompt below. Use the planning page to plan your writing. Then write or type your answer.

Caroline was so excited she could hardly sleep. She had never traveled out of the state before. She was looking forward to the trip.

Write a story about Caroline's trip.

Hint

The writing prompt tells you that your story should be about a person taking a trip out of the state. Use this as the starting point and think of a story based around this idea. Think about where Caroline might be going and what she might be doing there.

As you plan your story, think of a main event that will make your story interesting. Maybe the trip is not like she expected, maybe something goes wrong, or maybe she meets a fascinating person. Be creative and try to make your story interesting!

Planning Page

The Story
Write a summary of your story.

The Beginning
Describe what is going to happen at the start of your story.

The Middle
Describe what is going to happen in the middle of your story.

The End
Describe what is going to happen at the end of your story.

Task 4: Opinion Piece Writing Task

Directions: Read the writing prompt below. Use the planning page to plan your writing. Then write or type your answer.

Some people say that opposites attract. They think that people who are very different can get on very well.

Do you think that opposites attract? Why or why not? Use facts, details, or examples to support your opinion.

Hint

You may have several different opinions. Maybe you think that people who are different can disagree a lot, but can also challenge each other. Maybe you think it can be boring to spend time with someone who is just like you, but also think that it is good to have a friend with similar interests. A good composition will focus on one idea!

Choose one opinion and make that the focus of your essay. If you decide that opposites attract, think of two or three reasons you can use to show how people who are different benefit each other. If you decide that opposites do not attract, think of two or three problems that occur when two people are very different.

Planning Page

Summary
Write a brief summary of what you are going to write about.

Supporting Details
Write down the facts, details, or examples you are going to include.

Outline
Write a plan for what you are going to write. Include the main points you want to cover and the order you will cover them.

Writing and Editing Checklist

After you finish writing your opinion piece, you can use this guide to review and edit your work. Use the questions as a guide to finding ways you can improve your work.

Writing Checklist

- ✓ Does your work have one clear opinion?
- ✓ Does your work have a strong opening? Does the opening introduce the topic and state the opinion?
- ✓ Is your opinion supported? Have you used facts, details, and examples to support your opinion?
- ✓ Is your work well-organized? Is related information grouped together? Does each paragraph have one main idea?
- ✓ Do your ideas flow well? Have you used words and phrases to link ideas well?
- ✓ Does your work have a strong ending? Does the ending restate the main idea and tie up the opinion piece?

Editing Checklist

- ✓ Have you used a variety of sentence structures? Are your sentences all written correctly?
- ✓ Is the grammar correct?
- ✓ Are all words spelled correctly? You can check the spelling of any words you are not sure of.
- ✓ Is punctuation used correctly?
- ✓ If dialogue is used, is it punctuated correctly?
- ✓ Are all words capitalized correctly?

Reading and Writing

Practice Set 3

This practice set contains four writing tasks. These are described below.

Task 1: Short Passage with Questions

This task has a short passage followed by questions. Read each question carefully. Then write your answer in the space provided.

You can also practice writing skills by completing the Core Writing Skills Practice exercise.

Task 2: Short Passage with Questions

This task has a short passage followed by questions. Read each question carefully. Then write your answer in the space provided.

You can also practice writing skills by completing the Core Writing Skills Practice exercise.

Task 3: Long Passage with Essay Question

This task has a longer passage with an essay question. Read the passage, complete the planning page, and then write or type your answer.

Task 4: Personal Narrative Writing Task

This final task requires you to write a personal narrative. Read the writing prompt, complete the planning page, and then write or type your answer.

Task 1: Short Passage with Questions

Vacation Time

Quinn, Hoy, and Max were sitting beside the basketball court eating lunch.

"What are you doing this summer, Hoy?" Quinn asked.

"Well, I'll probably go to see my Grandma in Florida. What about you?" Hoy replied.

"That sounds like fun. I'm going to go visit my Dad in Australia!" Quinn said.

"What about you?" Quinn asked Max.

"I'm going to stay here in town," Max said.

Quinn and Hoy both said that it sounded a little boring.

Max tilted his head a little and thought for a moment.

"Well, I'm going to watch television, play basketball, make costumes, ride my bike, play computer games, read some books…"

Max went on and on and listed even more things he was going to do.

Quinn stared at Max, "Oh boy, is that all?"

The boys laughed and ate the rest of their lunch.

CORE WRITING SKILLS PRACTICE
WRITE A PERSONAL NARRATIVE

In the story, Max makes the most of his vacation at home. Think of a time when you had to make the most of something. Write a narrative describing that time. Tell what you did to make the most of things.

1. How are Max's vacation plans different from Quinn's and Hoy's?

   Hint This question is asking you to compare Max's plans with Quinn's and Hoy's plans.

   _____
   _____
   _____
   _____

2. Do you think that Max's vacation plans sound interesting or dull? Use details from the passage in your answer.

   Hint This question is asking for your opinon. Make sure you use details from the passage to support your opinion.

   _____
   _____
   _____
   _____

Task 2: Short Passage with Questions

The Hobbit

Dear Diary,

Today I was reading an old book that my grandpa gave me called *The Hobbit*. We were talking about how I liked to read yesterday. He told me *The Hobbit* was his favorite book and gave me his copy out of the bookcase. So far the book has been pretty cool. I especially love the magical city that all the elves live in. It would be amazing if a place like that really existed.

I have always loved fantasy books. They allow you to visit an amazing new place that could never really exist! I love just being able to imagine such a magical place. I sometimes stop reading, close my eyes, and imagine that I live in a magical city. I think my grandpa does the same because he often falls asleep while he's reading!

Adam

CORE WRITING SKILLS PRACTICE
WRITE A SHORT STORY

Imagine that you find yourself lost in a magical forest. Answer the questions below to help plan a fantasy story. Then write your story.

What is the magical forest like?

_____

How do you find your way out of the magical forest?

_____

What happens in the end?

_____

1   Why do you think Adam's grandfather gave him *The Hobbit* to read?

Hint This question is asking you to make an inference. Use the information in the passage to draw your own conclusion.

_____

_____

_____

_____

_____

2   What does Adam like about fantasy books? Use details from the passage to support your answer.

_____

_____

_____

_____

_____

3 Adam says that he has always loved fantasy books. What type of books do you like the most? Explain why you like those types of books.

> **Hint:** Some common genres include science fiction, mystery, adventure, drama, and comedy. Choose a genre that you like and explain what you like about it.

_____

_____

_____

_____

_____

_____

_____

_____

_____

_____

_____

_____

Writing and Editing Checklist

After you finish writing your answer to question 3, you can use this guide to review and edit your work. Use the questions as a guide to finding ways you can improve your work.

Writing Checklist

- ✓ Does your work have a strong opening? Does it introduce the topic and the main ideas?
- ✓ Is your work well-organized? Is related information grouped together? Does each paragraph have one main idea?
- ✓ Have you clearly explained what you like about the genre you chose?
- ✓ Is your work focused? Are there any details that do not fit with your main ideas?
- ✓ Do your ideas flow well? Have you used words and phrases to link ideas well?

Editing Checklist

- ✓ Have you used a variety of sentence structures? Are your sentences all written correctly?
- ✓ Is the grammar correct?
- ✓ Are all words spelled correctly? You can check the spelling of any words you are not sure of.
- ✓ Is punctuation used correctly?
- ✓ If dialogue is used, is it punctuated correctly?
- ✓ Are all words capitalized correctly?

Task 3: Long Passage with Essay Question

Directions: Read the passage below. Then answer the question that follows. Use the planning page to plan your writing. Then write or type your essay.

The Super Bowl

The Super Bowl is the deciding game of the National Football League (NFL). It decides who wins the championship trophy each season. It was first played in the winter of 1967 to determine the champion of the 1966 season.

At the time it was created, there were two American football leagues. These were the NFL and the AFL, or American Football League. The winners of each league would play against each other to determine which team was the overall champion.

When the two leagues merged, the game was retained. It has since become a game where the top national teams play each other for the main championship. The Green Bay Packers won the first two Super Bowls played in 1967 and 1968. They were considered to be the best team at the time. Many people thought they would continue to win for years to come. This changed in 1969 when the New York Jets won Super Bowl III. This was the last Super Bowl that included teams from separate NFL and AFL leagues.

The game has grown steadily in popularity since this time. It is played annually on a Sunday. The timing of the game has changed since 1970. While it used to be played in early January, it is now played on the first Sunday in February. The Super Bowl game has become a major part of America's culture. It is even a national holiday across the nation.

The team that wins the Super Bowl receives the Vince Lombardi Trophy. It is named after the coach of the Green Bay Packers who won the initial Super Bowl games. The Super Bowl has emerged as the most watched television event in America. Super Bowl XLV was played in 2011 and drew a national audience of more than 110 million viewers. The Super Bowl is also one of the most watched sporting events throughout the world. Only the UEFA Champions League trophy in soccer is viewed by a higher global audience.

The Pittsburgh Steelers have won a total of six Super Bowls. They stand alone as the most successful team in the contest's history. The Dallas Cowboys and the San Francisco 49ers have each won the trophy five times. The Pittsburgh Steelers had a chance to win a seventh title in the 2011 Super Bowl. However, they were defeated by the Green Bay Packers. It was the fourth win for the Green Bay Packers.

Nation (NFL) →

1. Write a summary of the information in the passage about the Green Bay Packers. Use details from the passage in your answer.

In your answer, be sure to
- summarize the information about the Green Bay Packers
- use details from the passage in your answer
- write an answer of between 1 and 2 pages

Hint

The passage includes many details about the Super Bowl. In your answer, you need to focus on only summarizing the information given about the Green Bay Packers. As you plan your writing, divide the information given into subtopics. For example, you might describe their early success, then the influence of their first coach, and then end with recent events.

Planning Page

Summary

Write a brief summary of what you are going to write about.

Supporting Details

Write down the facts, details, or examples you are going to include in your answer.

Outline

Write a plan for what you are going to write. Include the main points you want to cover and the order you will cover them.

Task 4: Personal Narrative Writing Task

Directions: Read the writing prompt below. Use the planning page to plan your writing. Then write or type your answer.

Rainy days can be boring because you are stuck indoors. Think about a time when you had to spend the day indoors.

Write a composition describing a time when you had to spend the day indoors. Describe what you did for the day.

Hint

Stay focused! You might be able to think of several times that you could write about, but don't try to write about them all. Instead, choose just one day and write about that day in detail.

Your answer should describe the day. You should include many details that will help the reader imagine what you did for the day. You could also include details about how you felt during the day.

Planning Page

Summary

Write a brief summary of what you are going to write about.

Outline

Write a plan for what you are going to write. Include the main points you want to cover and the order you will cover them.

Writing and Editing Checklist

After you finish writing your personal narrative, you can use this guide to review and edit your work. Use the questions as a guide to finding ways you can improve your work.

Writing Checklist

- ✓ Does your work have a strong opening? Does it introduce the main ideas or set the scene well?
- ✓ Is your work well-organized? Is related information grouped together? Does each paragraph have one main idea?
- ✓ Does your work have an effective ending? Does it tie up the events well?
- ✓ Is your work focused? Are there any details that do not fit with your main ideas?
- ✓ Do your ideas flow well? Have you used words and phrases to link ideas well?
- ✓ Have you used strong words? Are there words that could be replaced with better ones?
- ✓ Have you used effective descriptions? Could your descriptions be improved?
- ✓ Have you used sensory details? Could you add more sensory details to help readers imagine the scene?

Editing Checklist

- ✓ Have you used a variety of sentence structures? Are your sentences all written correctly?
- ✓ Is the grammar correct?
- ✓ Are all words spelled correctly? You can check the spelling of any words you are not sure of.
- ✓ Is punctuation used correctly?
- ✓ If dialogue is used, is it punctuated correctly?
- ✓ Are all words capitalized correctly?

Reading and Writing

Practice Set 4

This practice set contains four writing tasks. These are described below.

Task 1: Short Passage with Questions

This task has a short passage followed by questions. Read each question carefully. Then write your answer in the space provided.

You can also practice writing skills by completing the Core Writing Skills Practice exercise.

Task 2: Short Passage with Questions

This task has a short passage followed by questions. Read each question carefully. Then write your answer in the space provided.

You can also practice writing skills by completing the Core Writing Skills Practice exercise.

Task 3: Opinion Piece Writing Task

This task requires you to write an opinion piece. Read the writing prompt, complete the planning page, and then write or type your answer.

Task 4: Short Story Writing Task

This task requires you to write a short story. Read the writing prompt, complete the planning page, and then write or type your answer.

Task 1: Short Passage with Questions

Not So Simple

The donkey was wandering across the farmstead. All of a sudden, he heard the chirp of a grasshopper. The donkey was enchanted and followed the sound until he saw the grasshopper.

"What sort of food do you live off to have such a wonderful melody?" the donkey asked the grasshopper.

"I live off the dew," the grasshopper replied, before hopping away quickly.

The donkey had nothing but dew for weeks. He still didn't sound anything like the grasshopper. He was also starting to feel very ill. He started chewing on some grass to get his energy back.

"I guess it's not that simple," said the donkey.

CORE WRITING SKILLS PRACTICE

What does the illustration suggest about how the donkey feels at the end of the passage? Why does the donkey feel that way?

_____

_____

_____

_____

_____

1 Write a summary of the events of the passage.

> **Hint** A summary should describe the main events of a passage. It should include only the important events or details.

_____

_____

_____

_____

_____

2 What is the main theme of the passage? Use details from the passage to support your answer.

_____

_____

_____

_____

_____

Task 2: Short Passage with Questions

The Deepest of Deeps

The Mariana Trench is a natural sinkhole in the ocean floor. It is over 35,000 feet deep and is found in the western Pacific Ocean, to the east of the Mariana Islands. If you were to put Mount Everest in this trench, you would still have about 6000 feet of water above it!

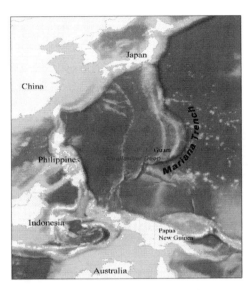

The trench forms at a point where tectonic plates meet. Tectonic plates are large slabs of rock that make up the Earth's crust. Tectonic plates are always slowly moving. At points where plates meet, trenches or mountains can form and events like volcanoes and earthquakes often occur. What happens at the meeting point depends on how the plates are moving. They could be moving away from each other, moving toward each other, or sliding across each other.

In the Mariana Trench, two plates meet and one plate moves under the other. A large valley forms as one plate sinks into the Earth. The very bottom of the trench is the deepest part of the ocean.

CORE WRITING SKILLS PRACTICE		
The word *deepest* includes the suffix *-est*. The word *deepest* means "the most deep." Write **three** more words with the suffix *-est* and their meanings below.		
Word		**Meaning**

1 What is the main purpose of the information about Mount Everest?

_____

_____

_____

_____

_____

2 How did the Mariana Trench form? Use details from the passage to support your answer.

Hint — Make sure you do not write exactly what is in the passage. Describe how the trench formed in your own words.

_____

_____

_____

_____

_____

Task 3: Opinion Piece Writing Task

Directions: Read the writing prompt below. Use the planning page to plan your writing. Then write or type your answer.

Read this quote about goals.

> A goal without a plan is just a wish.
> -Antoine de Saint-Exupery

Think about why planning is important. Write an opinion piece in which you explain to people why it is important to make plans to achieve your goals. Use facts, details, or examples in your answer.

Hint

This writing task introduces the topic with a quote. Start by thinking about what the quote means. It is describing the importance of planning and saying that you will not reach your goals unless you plan. In your writing, you should write about why planning is important.

Your answer can be based on your personal experience. You could describe how you achieved a goal by planning, how you always make plans, or how you failed to achieve a goal because you did not plan.

Planning Page

Summary
Write a brief summary of what you are going to write about.

Supporting Details
Write down the facts, details, or examples you are going to include.

Outline
Write a plan for what you are going to write. Include the main points you want to cover and the order you will cover them.

Task 4: Short Story Writing Task

Directions: Read the writing prompt below. Use the planning page to plan your writing. Then write or type your answer.

Kevin and Jane were going horse riding. Jane had never been before and was a little nervous.

Write a story about Kevin and Jane's horse ride.

> ### Hint
>
> A good story has a beginning, middle, and end. As you plan your story, focus on what is going to happen in each part.
>
> The beginning often introduces the characters and the setting. The start of this story might describe Kevin and Jane starting out on their horse ride.
>
> The middle of the story might describe what happens during the horse ride. This will be the main part of your story. It will usually be 2 or 3 paragraphs long. In this part, describe the events that take place. A good story will often have a main problem. For example, Jane might be afraid and might have to overcome her fear, or Jane's horse might race off.
>
> At the end of the story, the problem is usually solved. This ties up the story and makes it a complete story.

Planning Page

The Story
Write a summary of your story.

The Beginning
Describe what is going to happen at the start of your story.

The Middle
Describe what is going to happen in the middle of your story.

The End
Describe what is going to happen at the end of your story.

Writing and Editing Checklist

After you finish writing your story, you can use this guide to review and edit your work. Use the questions as a guide to finding ways you can improve your work.

Writing Checklist

- ✓ Does your story have a strong opening? Does it introduce the characters, the setting, or events well?
- ✓ Is your story well-organized? Do the events flow well?
- ✓ Does your story have an effective ending? Does it tie up the story well?
- ✓ Does your story include dialogue? If not, could dialogue make your story better?
- ✓ Have you used strong words? Are there words that could be replaced with better ones?
- ✓ Have you used effective descriptions? Could your descriptions be improved?
- ✓ Have you used sensory details? Could you add more sensory details to help readers imagine the scene?

Editing Checklist

- ✓ Have you used a variety of sentence structures? Are your sentences all written correctly?
- ✓ Is the grammar correct?
- ✓ Are all words spelled correctly? You can check the spelling of any words you are not sure of.
- ✓ Is punctuation used correctly?
- ✓ If dialogue is used, is it punctuated correctly?
- ✓ Are all words capitalized correctly?

Reading and Writing

Practice Set 5

This practice set contains four writing tasks. These are described below.

Task 1: Short Passage with Questions

This task has a short passage followed by questions. Read each question carefully. Then write your answer in the space provided.

You can also practice writing skills by completing the Core Writing Skills Practice exercise.

Task 2: Short Passage with Questions

This task has a short passage followed by questions. Read each question carefully. Then write your answer in the space provided.

You can also practice writing skills by completing the Core Writing Skills Practice exercise.

Task 3: Long Passage with Essay Question

This task has a longer passage with an essay question. Read the passage, complete the planning page, and then write or type your answer.

Task 4: Personal Narrative Writing Task

This final task requires you to write a personal narrative. Read the writing prompt, complete the planning page, and then write or type your answer.

Task 1: Short Passage with Questions

To the Moon

Most people know that we first walked on the Moon in 1969 with NASA's Apollo 11 mission. But did you know that the first human-made object to reach the surface of the Moon was the Soviet Union's Luna 2, in 1959?

NASA went on to make six manned landings between 1969 and 1972, with one mission failure. Fortunately, all astronauts safely returned home. Rocks from the Moon were collected for analysis during all manned and unmanned missions. Many scientists believe that we will one day be able to colonize the Moon.

The crew of the Apollo 11 mission were Neil Armstrong, Buzz Aldrin, and Michael Collins. Both Armstrong and Aldrin walked on the Moon.

CORE WRITING SKILLS PRACTICE

The word *colony* refers to a group of people who have settled an area. Based on this and its use in the passage, what does the word *colonize* mean?

_____

_____

_____

_____

_____

1 What is the main purpose of the first paragraph?

2 Which detail from the passage did you find most interesting or surprising? Explain why you found that detail interesting or surprising.

Task 2: Short Passage with Questions

Rex the Superhero

Rex walked the city with his head held high. His long red cape flowed off his back like flames dancing in the wind. The people were so happy to have such a big and strong hero. They would always wave to Rex and smile.

Rex was a young dinosaur who had always wanted to be a superhero when he grew up. He never thought about anything else. One day Rex chased down a man who stole a lady's purse. Sadly, Rex's ambitions were quickly forgotten when he realized that he was afraid. He had cornered the thief, but he was too afraid to take the purse back. His legs started shaking like jelly, and he was too afraid to even shout at the thief. Rex realized that being a hero might be harder than he had thought.

CORE WRITING SKILLS PRACTICE

The story has a third person point of view. Think about how the story would be different if it had a first person point of view. Describe what happens when Rex catches the thief from Rex's point of view. Be sure to describe how Rex feels.

_____

_____

_____

_____

_____

_____

1. Identify **two** similes used in the passage. Explain what each simile helps describe.

   Hint   A simile compares two things using the words *like* or *as*.

   1: _____

   _____

   _____

   2: _____

   _____

   _____

2. What happens when Rex catches the thief? What does Rex learn about himself?

   _____

   _____

   _____

   _____

   _____

3 What is Rex's main problem in the passage? How does his problem affect his goals? Use details from the passage in your answer.

Hint The passage describes what Rex's main goal in life is, and then shows that he has a problem that might stop him from achieving his goal.

_____

_____

_____

_____

_____

_____

_____

_____

_____

_____

_____

_____

Writing and Editing Checklist

After you finish writing your answer to question 3, you can use this guide to review and edit your work. Use the questions as a guide to finding ways you can improve your work.

Writing Checklist

- ✓ Does your work have a strong opening? Does it introduce the topic and the main ideas?
- ✓ Is your work well-organized? Is related information grouped together? Does each paragraph have one main idea?
- ✓ Have you clearly explained what Rex's problem is and how it affects him?
- ✓ Have you used details from the passage to support your claims?
- ✓ Is your work focused? Are there any details that do not fit with your main ideas?
- ✓ Do your ideas flow well? Have you used words and phrases to link ideas well?

Editing Checklist

- ✓ Have you used a variety of sentence structures? Are your sentences all written correctly?
- ✓ Is the grammar correct?
- ✓ Are all words spelled correctly? You can check the spelling of any words you are not sure of.
- ✓ Is punctuation used correctly?
- ✓ If dialogue is used, is it punctuated correctly?
- ✓ Are all words capitalized correctly?

Task 3: Long Passage with Essay Question

Directions: Read the passage below. Then answer the question that follows. Use the planning page to plan your writing. Then write or type your essay.

A New Arrival

Dear Diary,

Today was a very exciting day for me and my family. It was the day that my new baby brother came home from the hospital. He was born yesterday morning at 9:51 am. My father came home in the afternoon and was overjoyed. He weighed 8 pounds and 1 ounce and my parents named him Bradley. My dad says that he is the most beautiful baby. I could barely sleep the night before. I was so excited about Bradley coming home. Eventually, I drifted off to sleep just as the morning sun began to rise.

I woke up as usual today at 9:00 am. I went downstairs and enjoyed some toast for breakfast. I knew that my father was collecting my mother and Bradley at 11:00 am. I watched TV for a while before trying to read one of my favorite books. Whatever I tried to do, I just could not take my mind off my newborn brother. I couldn't help but try to imagine what he must look like. In my mind, he had bright blond hair and sparkling blue eyes. I wondered whether he would understand who I was when he first saw me. My daydreaming was interrupted by my dad's voice. It was finally time to leave.

I headed out to the car and we drove towards the hospital. I couldn't stop talking as we made our way through the winding roads. The short trip to the hospital seemed to take forever. We finally arrived at the hospital. We made our way through the reception and headed to the maternity ward. As we arrived at the doors, I could see my mother at the far end. She held a small bundle wrapped in a blue blanket in her arms.

Mum just smiled as I reached the end of her bed. She looked tired but extremely happy. I just stared for a few moments before Mom asked me if I wanted to meet my brother! I couldn't stop smiling and reached out in an instant. Mom held out her arms and passed Bradley to me. I took him in my arms and held his tiny little baby body close to my chest. As I looked down, he opened his eyes and looked at me. They were the deepest blue that anyone could ever imagine. As I stroked his face he began to smile softly. Dad told me that he looks just like me when I was born. The thought that I was ever that beautiful made me smile. Then Bradley slowly closed his eyes and drifted off to sleep.

Bye for now,

Emma

1 How does Emma feel about having a new baby brother? Use details from the passage to support your answer.

In your answer, be sure to
- describe how Emma feels about having a new baby brother
- use details from the passage to support your answer
- write an answer of between 1 and 2 pages

Hint

The key to receiving full marks for this question is to support your answer well. You can tell from the passage that Emma is happy or excited about having a new baby brother. Use this as the introduction of your essay.

Then write a few paragraphs giving details from the passage that show that she is happy or excited. Finally, end your answer with a conclusion.

The conclusion should be a 1-paragraph summary of how she feels and how you can tell.

Planning Page

Summary
Write a brief summary of what you are going to write about.

Supporting Details
Write down the facts, details, or examples you are going to include in your answer.

Outline
Write a plan for what you are going to write. Include the main points you want to cover and the order you will cover them.

Task 4: Personal Narrative Writing Task

Directions: Read the writing prompt below. Use the planning page to plan your writing. Then write or type your answer.

The Speech

I have to calm my shaking hands.
I have to hide my shaking knees.
I have to think only good thoughts,
And whisper "please go well, please."

In "The Speech," the poet describes how he has to be brave when he is about to give a speech. Think of a time when you had to be brave. How did you find a way to be brave? Write a composition about a situation where you had to be brave.

Hint

This writing task introduces the topic by using a poem. You do not have to refer to the poem in your answer. The poem is just there to help you start thinking about the topic.

The goal of your writing is to write about a time when you had to be brave. It could be when you had to give a speech, or it could be in any other situation that scared you. Maybe you're scared of heights and have to be brave every time you're in a tall building, or maybe you're scared of snakes and have to be brave when you are hiking. Focus on what makes you scared and how you overcome your fear.

Planning Page

Summary
Write a brief summary of what you are going to write about.

Outline
Write a plan for what you are going to write. Include the main points you want to cover and the order you will cover them.

Writing and Editing Checklist

After you finish writing your personal narrative, you can use this guide to review and edit your work. Use the questions as a guide to finding ways you can improve your work.

Writing Checklist

- ✓ Does your work have a strong opening? Does it introduce the main ideas or set the scene well?
- ✓ Is your work well-organized? Is related information grouped together? Does each paragraph have one main idea?
- ✓ Does your work have an effective ending? Does it tie up the events well?
- ✓ Is your work focused? Are there any details that do not fit with your main ideas?
- ✓ Do your ideas flow well? Have you used words and phrases to link ideas well?
- ✓ Have you used strong words? Are there words that could be replaced with better ones?
- ✓ Have you used effective descriptions? Could your descriptions be improved?
- ✓ Have you used sensory details? Could you add more sensory details to help readers imagine the scene?

Editing Checklist

- ✓ Have you used a variety of sentence structures? Are your sentences all written correctly?
- ✓ Is the grammar correct?
- ✓ Are all words spelled correctly? You can check the spelling of any words you are not sure of.
- ✓ Is punctuation used correctly?
- ✓ If dialogue is used, is it punctuated correctly?
- ✓ Are all words capitalized correctly?

Reading and Writing

Practice Set 6

This practice set contains four writing tasks. These are described below.

Task 1: Short Passage with Questions

This task has a short passage followed by questions. Read each question carefully. Then write your answer in the space provided.

You can also practice writing skills by completing the Core Writing Skills Practice exercise.

Task 2: Short Passage with Questions

This task has a short passage followed by questions. Read each question carefully. Then write your answer in the space provided.

You can also practice writing skills by completing the Core Writing Skills Practice exercise.

Task 3: Short Story Writing Task

This task requires you to write a short story. Read the writing prompt, complete the planning page, and then write or type your answer.

Task 4: Opinion Piece Writing Task

This final task requires you to write an opinion piece. Read the writing prompt, complete the planning page, and then write or type your answer.

Task 1: Short Passage with Questions

The Race

Sean's go-kart roared around the racing track and started to thunder down the hill. Benny had been behind Sean the entire way. Benny kept driving down the hill safely and steadily behind Sean. The final corner was coming up and Sean looked behind him.

"Ha! You'll never catch me," Sean said.

He slammed his foot down on the gas. The go-kart leapt forward. It flew into the final corner.

Sean was going so fast around the corner that his go-kart spun out. He landed backwards against the wall of tires on the side of the track. Benny waved to Sean as he drove by and won the race.

CORE WRITING SKILLS PRACTICE
WRITE A SHORT STORY

Think of another situation where going slow and steady might lead to better results than going fast. Answer the questions below to help plan your story. Then write a short story that has the same message as "The Race."

What situation are you writing about?

___

How does going slow and steady help someone do better?

___

What happens because someone is going too fast?

___

1 How is the way Sean drives different from the way Benny drives?

Hint — This question is asking you to compare two characters and describe how they are different.

_____

_____

_____

_____

2 Identify **two** words the author uses to help the reader imagine Sean's go-kart. Describe the image created by each word.

Hint — The author has selected words that help the reader imagine how fast Sean is going. Identify two of these words.

_____

_____

_____

_____

Task 2: Short Passage with Questions

Come Sail Away

Steven pushed the sail and the boat began to slowly turn. Looking off into the distance, all he could see was water. Steven enjoyed his adventures out to sea. He often spent the entire day on his sailboat. He especially enjoyed it when his son and daughter joined him. Kendra, Steven's wife, was scared of the water so she didn't let the kids go sailing much.

As Steven turned the boat to sail toward an island, he wished his kids were with him today. He imagined how excited his daughter would be. She would probably be staring out into the water looking for dolphins or turtles. He thought about how much his son loved learning how to sail. He would probably be helping Steven sail the boat. Steven sighed sadly. Spending a long day out at sea always left him with mixed feelings.

CORE WRITING SKILLS PRACTICE

Describe **two** ways the day would be different if Steven had his son and daughter with him.

_____

_____

_____

_____

_____

1. How does Steven most likely feel about sailing on his own? Use details from the passage in your answer.

_____
_____
_____
_____
_____

2. Do you think going sailing with Steven would be exciting or relaxing? Use details from the passage to support your answer.

Hint: This question is asking for your personal opinion. You could answer with either opinion. But make sure you explain why you have that opinion.

_____
_____
_____
_____
_____

Task 3: Short Story Writing Task

Directions: Read the writing prompt below. Use the planning page to plan your writing. Then write or type your answer.

Look at the picture below.

Write a story based on what is happening in the picture.

Your story should be based on the picture given. You should use the picture to come up with an idea for your story. The story shows a group of people about to start a race. You could base your story on a character competing in the race, someone watching the race, or even an athletics coach.

The key to writing a good story based on a picture is not to focus on describing what is happening in the picture. Instead, use the picture as a general idea, and make sure you come up with a complete story based on a race.

Planning Page

The Story
Write a summary of your story.

The Beginning
Describe what is going to happen at the start of your story.

The Middle
Describe what is going to happen in the middle of your story.

The End
Describe what is going to happen at the end of your story.

Task 4: Opinion Piece Writing Task

Directions: Read the writing prompt below. Use the planning page to plan your writing. Then write or type your answer.

Read this proverb about problems.

> A problem shared is a problem halved.

Do you agree with this proverb? Explain why or why not. Use facts, details, or examples in your answer.

Hint

A proverb is a short saying that states an idea. The idea in this proverb is that it is good to share your problems. You have to explain whether or not you agree with this.

When you are asked whether or not you agree with something, you will not be scored based on whether you agree or not. You will be scored on how well you explain why you do or do not agree. Don't worry about choosing the right answer. Instead, focus on what your personal opinion is. Then focus on clearly explaining why this is your opinion.

Planning Page

Summary
Write a brief summary of what you are going to write about.

Supporting Details
Write down the facts, details, or examples you are going to include.

Outline
Write a plan for what you are going to write. Include the main points you want to cover and the order you will cover them.

Writing and Editing Checklist

After you finish writing your opinion piece, you can use this guide to review and edit your work. Use the questions as a guide to finding ways you can improve your work.

Writing Checklist

- ✓ Does your work have one clear opinion?
- ✓ Does your work have a strong opening? Does the opening introduce the topic and state the opinion?
- ✓ Is your opinion supported? Have you used facts, details, and examples to support your opinion?
- ✓ Is your work well-organized? Is related information grouped together? Does each paragraph have one main idea?
- ✓ Do your ideas flow well? Have you used words and phrases to link ideas well?
- ✓ Does your work have a strong ending? Does the ending restate the main idea and tie up the opinion piece?

Editing Checklist

- ✓ Have you used a variety of sentence structures? Are your sentences all written correctly?
- ✓ Is the grammar correct?
- ✓ Are all words spelled correctly? You can check the spelling of any words you are not sure of.
- ✓ Is punctuation used correctly?
- ✓ If dialogue is used, is it punctuated correctly?
- ✓ Are all words capitalized correctly?

Reading and Writing

Practice Set 7

This practice set contains four writing tasks. These are described below.

Task 1: Short Passage with Questions

This task has a short passage followed by questions. Read each question carefully. Then write your answer in the space provided.

You can also practice writing skills by completing the Core Writing Skills Practice exercise.

Task 2: Short Passage with Questions

This task has a short passage followed by questions. Read each question carefully. Then write your answer in the space provided.

You can also practice writing skills by completing the Core Writing Skills Practice exercise.

Task 3: Long Passage with Essay Question

This task has a longer passage with an essay question. Read the passage, complete the planning page, and then write or type your answer.

Task 4: Explanatory Writing Task

This final task requires you to write an essay that explains something. Read the writing prompt, complete the planning page, and then write or type your answer.

Task 1: Short Passage with Questions

Clear Blue Sky

Do you know why the sky is blue? It's caused by the sunlight! But sunlight isn't blue, you might say. Well, sunlight is actually many different colors. But all of these colors are only seen at different wavelengths. Red and orange have the longest wavelength of the colors. Yellow and green have medium wavelengths, and blue has the shortest.

In normal conditions, the gas particles in our atmosphere scatter shorter wavelength colors much easier than the longer ones. The shorter wavelengths, like blue, are scattered more. This results in a beautiful blue sky.

CORE WRITING SKILLS PRACTICE

Describe the author's main purpose in the passage.

_____

_____

_____

Who do you think the main audience of the passage is meant to be? Explain how you can tell.

_____

_____

_____

_____

1. The passage describes how sunlight is made up of many different colors. Compare the wavelengths of the different colors.

_____
_____
_____
_____
_____

2. Explain why the sky appears blue.

Hint: Make sure you do not write exactly what is in the passage word for word. You should summarize what the passage tells you about why the sky is blue.

_____
_____
_____
_____
_____

Task 2: Short Passage with Questions

Harm's Diary

Dear Diary,

It's a Saturday and that means no school. So I decided to feed my brain for the day. This morning I started reading through an encyclopedia. Mostly, I was just flipping to random pages, but it was fun. They have always fascinated me with how much information is in them. I enjoyed reading about Scotland, badgers, and a writer named Aldous Huxley. Oh, I also read all about the first President of the United States, George Washington. It might sound like a boring day to some people, but I actually had a good time! I learned a lot of new things and I want to learn even more. Well, I better get to sleep.

See you tomorrow,

Harmanie

CORE WRITING SKILLS PRACTICE

The passage states that George Washington was the first American president. Use the Internet to find the first ten American presidents. List the first ten American presidents in order and the year each one became president.

1. *George Washington, 1789*
2. _____
3. _____
4. _____
5. _____
6. _____
7. _____
8. _____
9. _____
10. _____

1. What does Harmanie mean when she says that she decided to "feed her brain"?

   Hint Harmanie does not mean that she actually fed her brain. You have to work out what she is describing when she says this.

   _____

   _____

   _____

   _____

   _____

2. Give **two** details from the passage that show that Harmanie is a curious person.

   1: _____

   _____

   2: _____

   _____

Task 3: Long Passage with Essay Question

Directions: Read the passage below. Then answer the question that follows. Use the planning page to plan your writing. Then write or type your essay.

The Aspiring Star

Troy longed to be a professional basketball player. He had loved the sport ever since he was a small child. He was also very skilled and fast on the basketball court. Despite this, he had one small problem. He was very short. His school coach had suggested that he would never make it in the professional leagues. Although he was devastated at first, he refused to give up on his dream.

Troy had several trials at professional clubs but failed to earn a contract. It was then that he attended the training ground of the Los Angeles Lakers. He asked the coach for a trial. As usual, he was refused.

"But you haven't even given me a chance," said Troy.

"Why should I give you a shot?" asked the coach.

Troy paused before he answered.

"Because one day I am going to be the best player in the world and I will be able to help you out," he replied seriously.

The coach smiled at the confidence of the answer.

"Alright kid," he said. "I'll give you a chance to impress me."

Troy took part in a short practice match and was then allowed to showcase his individual skills. He was one of the most skillful players on show and had the will to win to match. The coach was stunned.

"You certainly have a lot of talent for a little fellow," he said. "How would you like to sign on a youth contract?"

Troy agreed and was soon rising through the ranks. Although some players thought he was too short to play, they soon changed their minds when they saw him in action. After two short years, he was a regular for the Lakers and had even won the award as the team's most valuable player. Even with Troy's help, the team was struggling. They were not winning many games and there were rumors that the coach was close to losing his job. It was before a game against the New York Jets that he called Troy into his office for a discussion.

"I have heard that if we lose tonight then I will be replaced as coach," he told Troy. "I need you to do more than play well tonight. I need you to carry the team and win the game. Do you remember your promise before I signed you?"

Troy nodded and smiled at his coach.

"You bet I do coach," he replied. "You bet I do."

Troy went on to play the game of his life that evening. The Lakers won the game and won every game that was left that season. The coach kept his job and led his team on to success.

1   The passage describes a boy who overcomes a barrier and achieves a personal goal. Think of a time when you had to overcome a barrier to achieve a goal. Describe that time.

In your answer, be sure to
- describe what your goal was
- describe what the barrier was
- describe how you overcame the barrier
- describe how it felt to overcome the barrier
- use details from the passage in your answer
- write an answer of between 1 and 2 pages

The question asks you to relate to the passage. You have to write about your own experience in overcoming a barrier. You will mainly use your own experience in your essay. However, you should still mention Troy's experience once or twice. For example, you might have been determined like Troy was. You could refer to Troy when you explain how determined you were.

Planning Page

Summary
Write a brief summary of what you are going to write about.

Supporting Details
Write down the facts, details, or examples you are going to include in your answer.

Outline
Write a plan for what you are going to write. Include the main points you want to cover and the order you will cover them.

Task 4: Explanatory Writing Task

Directions: Read the writing prompt below. Use the planning page to plan your writing. Then write or type your answer.

Many people like to collect things. Some people collect dolls. Other people collect stamps or baseball cards. What do you collect, or what would you like to collect?

Write an essay describing what you collect or what you would like to collect. In your essay, explain why you have chosen that item.

Hint

When planning your writing, it is a good idea to break down what you want to say into paragraphs. This will help make sure your writing is well-organized and easy to understand. In your outline, describe what you are going to cover in each paragraph. Make sure that each paragraph has one main idea.

The first paragraph should introduce the topic by telling what item you collect.

The middle part should explain why you have chosen that item. You might describe why it means something to you, why you enjoy collecting it, or what you do with your collection. This should be organized into two or three paragraphs that each have a main idea.

The final paragraph should sum up your main ideas.

Planning Page

Summary
Write a brief summary of what you are going to write about.

Outline
Write a plan for what you are going to write. Include the main points you want to cover and the order you will cover them.

Writing and Editing Checklist

After you finish writing your essay, you can use this guide to review and edit your work. Use the questions as a guide to finding ways you can improve your work.

Writing Checklist

- ✓ Does your work have a strong opening? Does it introduce the topic and the main ideas?
- ✓ Is your work well-organized? Is related information grouped together? Does each paragraph have one main idea?
- ✓ Have you included facts, details, and examples to support your ideas?
- ✓ Is your work focused? Are there any details that do not fit with your main ideas?
- ✓ Do your ideas flow well? Have you used words and phrases to link ideas well?
- ✓ Does your work have a strong ending?

Editing Checklist

- ✓ Have you used a variety of sentence structures? Are your sentences all written correctly?
- ✓ Is the grammar correct?
- ✓ Are all words spelled correctly? You can check the spelling of any words you are not sure of.
- ✓ Is punctuation used correctly?
- ✓ Are all words capitalized correctly?

Reading and Writing

Practice Set 8

This practice set contains four writing tasks. These are described below.

Task 1: Short Passage with Questions

This task has a short passage followed by questions. Read each question carefully. Then write your answer in the space provided.

You can also practice writing skills by completing the Core Writing Skills Practice exercise.

Task 2: Short Passage with Questions

This task has a short passage followed by questions. Read each question carefully. Then write your answer in the space provided.

You can also practice writing skills by completing the Core Writing Skills Practice exercise.

Task 3: Opinion Piece Writing Task

This task requires you to write an opinion piece. Read the writing prompt, complete the planning page, and then write or type your answer.

Task 4: Short Story Writing Task

This task requires you to write a short story. Read the writing prompt, complete the planning page, and then write or type your answer.

Task 1: Short Passage with Questions

Volcanoes

Hot magma and gases build up inside our Earth's crust. Every now and then, it bursts out from under the Earth's surface. The result is a volcano.

Think of a volcano as the Earth relieving internal pressure. When a volcano blows, rocks and ash are thrown out high into the atmosphere. Hot magma flows out of a volcano like a river. Magma above the Earth's surface is called lava. If you touched lava with a steel rod, it would melt in seconds. As it moves across the land, it even melts the rock underneath it.

This image shows the eruption of Mount Pinatubo in the Philippines in 1991. It was the second largest eruption of the twentieth century.

CORE WRITING SKILLS PRACTICE
WRITE A RESEARCH REPORT

Mount Vesuvius was one of the largest volcanic eruptions in history. Research and write a report about Mount Vesuvius. Use the questions below to guide you.

Where is Mount Vesuvius located?

When did the biggest eruption occur?

How great was the eruption?

Is Mount Vesuvius still erupting today?

1. Write a definition of the terms *magma* and *lava*.

   Hint: Use the information in the passage to write a brief definition of each term.

   Magma: _____

   _____

   Lava: _____

   _____

2. Why does the author most likely describe how lava would melt a steel rod in seconds?

   _____

   _____

   _____

   _____

   _____

   _____

Task 2: Short Passage with Questions

Dangerous Dreams

Filbert the elf sat and stared into the pond.

"I wish I was a grown up," he sighed. "Then I too could hunt with a bow and arrow."

Filbert had always sat and enjoyed watching his father on hunting trips. He looked forward to the day when he could hunt too.

"One day I'm going to hunt a wild dragon!" Filbert told his father.

His father chuckled. "Oh, Filbert! I think you're aiming a bit too high," he said.

Filbert's brow furrowed. "I'm going to be a dragon hunter if it's the last thing I do," Filbert said.

His father smiled and rocked in his chair.

"Yes, son," he said.

CORE WRITING SKILLS PRACTICE

How do you think Filbert feels about being too young to hunt? Explain.

_____

_____

_____

_____

_____

1 How can you tell that the events in the passage could not really happen?

Hint — The events in the passage are made-up and could not happen in real life. Explain how you can tell this.

_____

_____

_____

_____

2 How does Filbert's father most likely feel about Filbert's plans to hunt a dragon?

Hint — You should use the information in the passage to guess how Filbert's father feels.

_____

_____

_____

_____

3 Filbert is told he is too young to go hunting. Think of a time when you were told that you were too young to do something. Describe that time. Include details about how you felt.

Hint: This question is asking you to relate to the story. You should describe a time in your life. You do not have to use details from the passage in your answer.

_____

_____

_____

_____

_____

_____

_____

_____

_____

_____

_____

_____

Writing and Editing Checklist

After you finish writing your answer to question 3, you can use this guide to review and edit your work. Use the questions as a guide to finding ways you can improve your work.

Writing Checklist

- ✓ Does your work have a strong opening? Does it introduce the main ideas or set the scene well?
- ✓ Is your work well-organized? Is related information grouped together? Does each paragraph have one main idea?
- ✓ Does your work have an effective ending? Does it tie up the events well?
- ✓ Is your work focused? Are there any details that do not fit with your main ideas?
- ✓ Do your ideas flow well? Have you used words and phrases to link ideas well?
- ✓ Have you used strong words? Are there words that could be replaced with better ones?
- ✓ Have you used effective descriptions? Could your descriptions be improved?
- ✓ Have you used sensory details? Could you add more sensory details to help readers imagine the scene?

Editing Checklist

- ✓ Have you used a variety of sentence structures? Are your sentences all written correctly?
- ✓ Is the grammar correct?
- ✓ Are all words spelled correctly? You can check the spelling of any words you are not sure of.
- ✓ Is punctuation used correctly?
- ✓ If dialogue is used, is it punctuated correctly?
- ✓ Are all words capitalized correctly?

Task 3: Opinion Piece Writing Task

Directions: Read the writing prompt below. Use the planning page to plan your writing. Then write or type your answer.

Think about your teachers. What do you think makes a good teacher? Use facts, details, or examples to support your opinion.

Hint

When completing these writing tasks, it is important to include supporting details. In some tasks, you can use facts. In a task like this, it is often better to use details and examples. Once you have decided what makes a good teacher, thinks of details and examples you can use to support your opinion. You could use details about one teacher or you could use details about several teachers.

Planning Page

Summary
Write a brief summary of what you are going to write about.

Supporting Details
Write down the facts, details, or examples you are going to include.

Outline
Write a plan for what you are going to write. Include the main points you want to cover and the order you will cover them.

Task 4: Short Story Writing Task

Directions: Read the writing prompt below. Use the planning page to plan your writing. Then write or type your answer.

Look at the picture below.

Write a story based on what is happening in the picture.

Hint

One way to improve your writing is to focus on how you describe things. You can choose words and phrases that make your writing more interesting. You can also use literary devices like similes. By describing things in a more interesting way, you will make your story more interesting to the reader.

Planning Page

The Story
Write a summary of your story.

The Beginning
Describe what is going to happen at the start of your story.

The Middle
Describe what is going to happen in the middle of your story.

The End
Describe what is going to happen at the end of your story.

Writing and Editing Checklist

After you finish writing your story, you can use this guide to review and edit your work. Use the questions as a guide to finding ways you can improve your work.

Writing Checklist

- ✓ Does your story have a strong opening? Does it introduce the characters, the setting, or events well?
- ✓ Is your story well-organized? Do the events flow well?
- ✓ Does your story have an effective ending? Does it tie up the story well?
- ✓ Does your story include dialogue? If not, could dialogue make your story better?
- ✓ Have you used strong words? Are there words that could be replaced with better ones?
- ✓ Have you used effective descriptions? Could your descriptions be improved?
- ✓ Have you used sensory details? Could you add more sensory details to help readers imagine the scene?

Editing Checklist

- ✓ Have you used a variety of sentence structures? Are your sentences all written correctly?
- ✓ Is the grammar correct?
- ✓ Are all words spelled correctly? You can check the spelling of any words you are not sure of.
- ✓ Is punctuation used correctly?
- ✓ If dialogue is used, is it punctuated correctly?
- ✓ Are all words capitalized correctly?

Reading and Writing

Practice Set 9

This practice set contains four writing tasks. These are described below.

Task 1: Short Passage with Questions

This task has a short passage followed by questions. Read each question carefully. Then write your answer in the space provided.

You can also practice writing skills by completing the Core Writing Skills Practice exercise.

Task 2: Short Passage with Questions

This task has a short passage followed by questions. Read each question carefully. Then write your answer in the space provided.

You can also practice writing skills by completing the Core Writing Skills Practice exercise.

Task 3: Long Passage with Essay Question

This task has a longer passage with an essay question. Read the passage, complete the planning page, and then write or type your answer.

Task 4: Explanatory Writing Task

This final task requires you to write an essay that explains something. Read the writing prompt, complete the planning page, and then write or type your answer.

Task 1: Short Passage with Questions

Easy Ice Cream

Making ice cream is easy. But be careful and remember to ask an adult for help when boiling the milk.

1. Put one cup of milk into a pot and bring it to a light boil.
2. Put one tablespoon of corn flour into a cup, add a splash of cold milk, and then mix.
3. Add this mixture to the pot and wait until the contents have become slightly thicker.
4. Mix eight tablespoons of sugar with one tablespoon of condensed milk. Then add to the pot and mix.
5. Allow the contents of the pot to cool before pouring into a mixing bowl.
6. Mix thoroughly, adding one cup of cream and one teaspoon of vanilla essence.
7. Now pour your mixture into a container and freeze it!

When it sets, it will be ready to share with your friends.

CORE WRITING SKILLS PRACTICE

Describe how the passage is organized. How does the way it is organized suit its purpose?

_____

_____

_____

_____

_____

1. What is the main purpose of the passage?

   Hint Passages have different purposes. The purpose of a passage could be to entertain, to persuade, to instruct or teach, or to explain.

   _____
   _____
   _____
   _____
   _____

2. Do you agree that ice cream would be easy to make? Explain why or why not.

   _____
   _____
   _____
   _____
   _____

Task 2: Short Passage with Questions

Going on a Picnic

I really love going for picnics in the park. Some days when I am bored I pack my basket and go by myself. I sit in the park and eat my sandwich. My favorite sandwiches to pack are egg and lettuce. I have loved egg and lettuce sandwiches ever since I was a kid.

After I eat, I enjoy watching the birds fly over and the people walk by. Sometimes I take a book with me and read a few chapters. I always enjoy just sitting by myself, enjoying the peace and quiet.

Other times, I go with my family. We all hang out together nibbling and chatting. These are good times too, but I really like the times I go on my own the best. Sometimes it's nice just to sit back, relax, and let your wind wander. I always come home feeling completely recharged.

CORE WRITING SKILLS PRACTICE

In the passage, the narrator describes how she likes going on picnics on her own. Think about how you do things on your own. What are some of the benefits of doing things on your own? What are some of the drawbacks?

_____

_____

_____

_____

_____

1. Complete the web below using information from the passage.

 When answering questions like this, make sure you use information that is given in the passage. Only list activities mentioned in the passage.

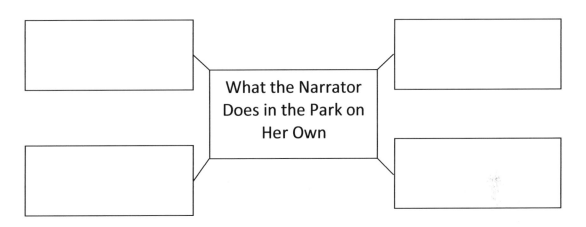

2. Circle the word below that best describes the narrator's time in the park. Then explain why you chose that word.

        relaxing   exciting

_____
_____
_____
_____
_____

Task 3: Long Passage with Essay Question

Directions: Read the passage below. Then answer the question that follows. Use the planning page to plan your writing. Then write or type your essay.

The Sahara Desert

The Sahara Desert is the world's largest subtropical desert. It covers most of North Africa. Its area is about 3.5 million square miles. This makes it almost as large as the United States of America. The Sahara Desert stretches all the way across Africa.

The Sahara Desert divides the continent of Africa into north and south. The southern border is marked by a savannah known as the Sahel. The land that lies to the south of the savannah is lush with more vegetation. The Sahara Desert features many large sand dunes. Some of these measure more than 600 feet from base to peak.

The Sahara Desert has been largely dry and with little plant life for more than 5,000 years. Before this time, it was far wetter than it is today. This allowed more plant life to thrive across its land. Thousands of ancient engravings have been found that show many types of river animals that have lived in the Sahara Desert. These have been found mainly in southeast Algeria. These suggest that crocodiles lived in the region at some point in time.

The climate of the Sahara Desert has also changed over several thousands of years. The area is also far smaller than it was during the last ice age. It was the end of the last ice age that brought a high level of rainfall to the Sahara. This was between 8000 and 6000 BC. Since this time, the northern part of the Sahara has gradually dried out. Though the southern Sahara still receives rain during monsoon season, it is still far less than years before. Some of the tallest mountain ranges occasionally receive snow peaks. The Tibetsi Mountains record some level of snowfall about once every seven years.

The modern era has seen several developments for the Sahara. One of these is that mines have been built to get the most from the natural resources within the region. There are also plans to build several highways across the Sahara. It is expected that one of these may be completed at some point in the future.

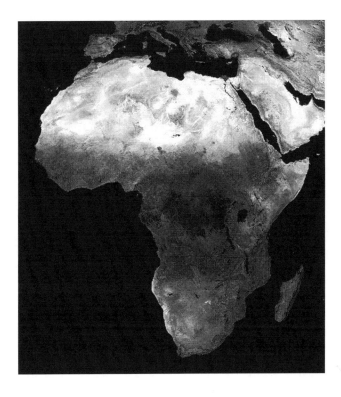

1   Even though life in the Sahara Desert is difficult, people do still live there. Describe **three** things that would make life in the Sahara Desert difficult. Use details from the passage in your answer.

In your answer, be sure to
- describe **three** things that would make life in the Sahara Desert difficult
- use details from the passage in your answer
- write an answer of between 1 and 2 pages

This question tells you to describe three things that would make life difficult. You might be able to think of more than three things. However, when a question tells you to write about a certain number of items, stick to that number. It is better to describe three things in detail than to list a large number of things. For each of the three things you choose, explain how that thing would make life difficult.

Planning Page

Summary
Write a brief summary of what you are going to write about.

Supporting Details
Write down the facts, details, or examples you are going to include in your answer.

Outline
Write a plan for what you are going to write. Include the main points you want to cover and the order you will cover them.

Task 4: Explanatory Writing Task

Directions: Read the writing prompt below. Use the planning page to plan your writing. Then write or type your answer.

Most people have one school subject that they like the most. What subject do you like the most? What do you like about that subject?

Write an essay describing what subject you like the most. In your essay, explain what you like about that subject.

Hint

When writing compositions like this, you will not be scored on what subject you like. Instead, you will be scored on how well you explain why you like that subject.

You should focus on giving 2 or 3 reasons that explain why you like that subject. There may be many more things that you like. However, it is better to describe 2 or 3 things in detail than to list many things you like.

When you write your plan, choose the 2 or 3 things you like most and write one paragraph about each thing.

Planning Page

Summary

Write a brief summary of what you are going to write about.

Outline

Write a plan for what you are going to write. Include the main points you want to cover and the order you will cover them.

Writing and Editing Checklist

After you finish writing your essay, you can use this guide to review and edit your work. Use the questions as a guide to finding ways you can improve your work.

Writing Checklist

- ✓ Does your work have a strong opening? Does it introduce the topic and the main ideas?
- ✓ Is your work well-organized? Is related information grouped together? Does each paragraph have one main idea?
- ✓ Have you included facts, details, and examples to support your ideas?
- ✓ Is your work focused? Are there any details that do not fit with your main ideas?
- ✓ Do your ideas flow well? Have you used words and phrases to link ideas well?
- ✓ Does your work have a strong ending?

Editing Checklist

- ✓ Have you used a variety of sentence structures? Are your sentences all written correctly?
- ✓ Is the grammar correct?
- ✓ Are all words spelled correctly? You can check the spelling of any words you are not sure of.
- ✓ Is punctuation used correctly?
- ✓ Are all words capitalized correctly?

Reading and Writing

Practice Set 10

This practice set contains four writing tasks. These are described below.

Task 1: Short Passage with Questions

This task has a short passage followed by questions. Read each question carefully. Then write your answer in the space provided.

You can also practice writing skills by completing the Core Writing Skills Practice exercise.

Task 2: Short Passage with Questions

This task has a short passage followed by questions. Read each question carefully. Then write your answer in the space provided.

You can also practice writing skills by completing the Core Writing Skills Practice exercise.

Task 3: Short Story Writing Task

This task requires you to write a short story. Read the writing prompt, complete the planning page, and then write or type your answer.

Task 4: Opinion Piece Writing Task

This final task requires you to write an opinion piece. Read the writing prompt, complete the planning page, and then write or type your answer.

Task 1: Short Passage with Questions

Submarines

The word *submarine* literally means "under the sea." It was originally called the submarine boat, but this was later shortened to just submarine. A submarine is a submersible vessel that can move underwater.

Submarines were originally powered by diesel engines. While submerged, they could only operate on battery power. This means they needed to surface periodically to charge their batteries, using their diesel engines. Modern submarines are mostly nuclear powered and do not need to surface to recharge.

Notes
Submersible – capable of being under water
Submerged – under water

This American submarine from the early 1900s was given the fitting name of the *USS Plunger*.

CORE WRITING SKILLS PRACTICE

The *USS Plunger* is one good name for a submarine. What is another good name for a submarine? Explain your choice.

_____

_____

_____

_____

1   According to the passage, why did submarines have to resurface often?

   _____
   _____
   _____
   _____
   _____

2   Describe **two** ways that submarines today are different than in the past.

   Hint You do not need to know anything extra about submarines to answer this question. All the details you need are in the passage.

   1: _____
   _____

   2: _____
   _____

Task 2: Short Passage with Questions

The Wolf

Wolves could once be found in abundance. They heavily populated Europe, Asia, North Africa, and North America. But as civilization became more and more widespread, wolves were culled to protect livestock and pets. Wolves are now a protected species in a lot of areas, especially in the United States. In other areas of the world, they are hunted for sport.

The name wolf usually refers to the gray wolf. Wolves live in close-knit families with a mated pair and their offspring, along with any other adopted wolves. DNA studies suggest that domestic dogs and wolves are closely related.

Some wolves look similar to dogs kept as family pets. But don't be fooled – wolves are wild creatures that have never been tamed. Wolves should never be approached.

CORE WRITING SKILLS PRACTICE

In some areas where wolves live close by, people have to be careful of wolves. Look up information on the Internet to find out how people can stay safe from wolves. Write **three** tips below for keeping safe from wolves.

1. _____

_____

2. _____

_____

3. _____

_____

1   Why did wolf numbers start to decrease? Use details from the passage in your answer.

_____

_____

_____

_____

_____

_____

2   Do you think wolf numbers will increase or decrease in the future? Use details from the passage to support your answer.

Hint: This question is asking you to make a prediction. Use the information in the passage to guess whether wolf numbers will continue to decrease or will start to increase again.

_____

_____

_____

_____

_____

_____

3 The passage describes how wolves are now protected. Do you think it is important to protect animal species that are decreasing in number? Explain why or why not.

Hint: Describe whether or not you think that animals should be protected. You can use information from the passage about wolves, as well as anything you know about other animals.

___
___
___
___
___
___
___
___
___
___
___
___
___

Writing and Editing Checklist

After you finish writing your answer to question 3, you can use this guide to review and edit your work. Use the questions as a guide to finding ways you can improve your work.

Writing Checklist

- ✓ Does your work have one clear opinion?
- ✓ Does your work have a strong opening? Does the opening introduce the topic and state the opinion?
- ✓ Is your opinion supported? Have you used facts, details, and examples to support your opinion?
- ✓ Have you used details from the passage to help support your answer?
- ✓ Is your work well-organized? Is related information grouped together? Does each paragraph have one main idea?
- ✓ Do your ideas flow well? Have you used words and phrases to link ideas well?
- ✓ Does your work have a strong ending? Does the ending restate the main idea and tie up the opinion piece.

Editing Checklist

- ✓ Have you used a variety of sentence structures? Are your sentences all written correctly?
- ✓ Is the grammar correct?
- ✓ Are all words spelled correctly? You can check the spelling of any words you are not sure of.
- ✓ Is punctuation used correctly?
- ✓ If dialogue is used, is it punctuated correctly?
- ✓ Are all words capitalized correctly?

Task 3: Short Story Writing Task

Directions: Read the writing prompt below. Use the planning page to plan your writing. Then write or type your answer.

Mary and Keith had been looking forward to the camping trip for weeks. But it didn't go quite as they had planned.

Write a story about Mary and Keith's camping trip.

Hint

One way to write a good story is to choose a style of writing and stick to it. The writing prompt for this story could be used to write a funny story, an adventure story, or a mystery story.

You should adjust how you write to suit the type of story you want to write. If you are writing a funny story, your writing might be casual and lighthearted. If you are writing a mystery story, you might want to make the reader curious. If you are writing an adventure story, you might want to make the events seem exciting.

Planning Page

The Story
Write a summary of your story.

The Beginning
Describe what is going to happen at the start of your story.

The Middle
Describe what is going to happen in the middle of your story.

The End
Describe what is going to happen at the end of your story.

Task 4: Opinion Piece Writing Task

Directions: Read the writing prompt below. Use the planning page to plan your writing. Then write or type your answer.

Read this piece of advice.

>Never judge a book by its cover.

Do you think this is good advice? Explain why or why not.

Hint

Start by thinking about what the advice means. It means that you should not judge people based only on appearance. Then think about whether you agree. Think about how this advice relates to your life.

A good essay will be focused, and will describe why you do or do not agree. Keep your essay focused by making sure that each paragraph you write has one main idea, and that all the ideas flow together. A good introduction and conclusion will also help tie the ideas together.

Planning Page

Summary
Write a brief summary of what you are going to write about.

Supporting Details
Write down the facts, details, or examples you are going to include.

Outline
Write a plan for what you are going to write. Include the main points you want to cover and the order you will cover them.

Writing and Editing Checklist

After you finish writing your opinion piece, you can use this guide to review and edit your work. Use the questions as a guide to finding ways you can improve your work.

Writing Checklist

- ✓ Does your work have one clear opinion?
- ✓ Does your work have a strong opening? Does the opening introduce the topic and state the opinion?
- ✓ Is your opinion supported? Have you used facts, details, and examples to support your opinion?
- ✓ Is your work well-organized? Is related information grouped together? Does each paragraph have one main idea?
- ✓ Do your ideas flow well? Have you used words and phrases to link ideas well?
- ✓ Does your work have a strong ending? Does the ending restate the main idea and tie up the opinion piece?

Editing Checklist

- ✓ Have you used a variety of sentence structures? Are your sentences all written correctly?
- ✓ Is the grammar correct?
- ✓ Are all words spelled correctly? You can check the spelling of any words you are not sure of.
- ✓ Is punctuation used correctly?
- ✓ If dialogue is used, is it punctuated correctly?
- ✓ Are all words capitalized correctly?

Answer Key

Developing Common Core Reading and Writing Skills

The state of New York has adopted the Common Core Learning Standards. Student learning throughout the year is based on these standards, and all the questions on the state tests assess these standards. All the questions and exercises in this workbook are based on the knowledge and skills described in the Common Core Learning Standards. While this workbook focuses specifically on the Common Core writing standards, the questions based on passages also assess Common Core reading standards.

Core Skills Practice Exercises

Each short passage in this workbook includes an exercise focused on one key skill described in the Common Core standards. The answer key identifies the core skill covered by each exercise, and describes what to look for in the student's response.

Scoring Constructed-Response Questions

The short passages in this workbook include constructed-response questions, where students provide a written answer to a question. Short questions are scored out of 2 and longer questions are scored out of 4. The answer key gives guidance on how to score these questions. Use the criteria listed as a guide to scoring these questions, and as a guide for giving the student advice on how to improve an answer.

Scoring Writing Tasks

The writing tasks in this workbook are scored based on rubrics that list the features expected of student writing. These features are based on the Common Core standards and are the same criteria used when scoring writing tasks on assessments. The rubrics used for scoring these questions are included in the back of this book. Use the rubric to score these questions, and as a guide for giving the student advice on how to improve an answer.

Practice Set 1

Task 1: Short Passage with Questions (Mystery Dish)

Core Writing Skills Practice

Core skill: Draw evidence from literary texts to support analysis, reflection, and research.

Answer: The student should refer to how Angelo does not want to eat the soup when he doesn't know what it is and relate this to the theme of being afraid of the unknown.

Q1. Give a score of 0, 1, or 2 based on how well the answer meets the criteria listed.
- It should make a reasonable prediction about what happens next.
- The prediction could be that Angelo eats the soup and enjoys it.
- The prediction should be supported by details in the passage.

Q2. Give a score of 0, 1, or 2 based on how well the answer meets the criteria listed.
- It should identify that the simile is when Angelo says that he is "as hungry as a bear in winter."
- It should explain that the simile means that Angelo is very hungry.

Task 2: Short Passage with Questions (The Amazing Amazon)

Core Writing Skills Practice

Core skill: Write informative/explanatory texts to examine a topic and convey ideas and information clearly.

Answer: Use the Informative/Explanatory Writing Rubric to give a score out of 4.

Q1. Give a score of 0, 1, or 2 based on how many boxes are correctly completed.
- The box for location should be completed as South America.
- The box for length should be completed as 4,000 miles.

Q2. Give a score of 0, 1, or 2 based on how well the answer meets the criteria listed.
- It should identify details from the passage that the student found interesting.
- It should include a brief explanation of why the student found the details interesting.

Task 3: Long Passage with Essay Question

Use the Informative/Explanatory Writing Rubric to review the work and give a score out of 4.

Task 4: Personal Narrative Writing Task

Use the Narrative Writing Rubric to review the work and give a score out of 4.

Practice Set 2

Task 1: Short Passage with Questions (The City of Troy)

Core Writing Skills Practice
Core skill: Determine the meaning of general academic and domain-specific words or phrases in a text relevant to a grade 4 topic or subject area.
Answer: The student should give a reasonable definition of each word.

Q1. Give a score of 0, 1, or 2 based on how well the answer meets the criteria listed.
- It should explain that the Greek warriors hid inside the wooden horse so they would be taken inside the gates.

Q2. Give a score of 0, 1, or 2 based on how well the answer meets the criteria listed.
- A complete answer should circle one of the words, and give a valid explanation of why the student made that choice.
- Both silly and clever could be correct answers, as long as the student explains the choice.
- The student could argue that hiding inside a giant horse is silly, or could argue that it is clever because it worked.

Task 2: Short Passage with Questions (Spiders)

Core Writing Skills Practice
Core skill: Draw evidence from literary texts to support analysis, reflection, and research.
Answer: The student should describe how it is ironic that the spider is scared of people when it is more common to think of people as being scared of spiders.

Q1. Give a score of 0, 1, or 2 based on how well the answer meets the criteria listed.
- It should describe how the spider says that it works hard all day and does not stop to play.

Q2. Give a score of 0, 1, or 2 based on how well the answer meets the criteria listed.
- It should describe how the second and fourth lines in each verse or stanza rhyme.

Task 3: Short Story Writing Task

Use the Narrative Writing Rubric to review the work and give a score out of 4.

Task 4: Opinion Piece Writing Task

Use the Opinion Writing Rubric to review the work and give a score out of 4.

Reading and Writing, Common Core Workbook, Grade 4

Practice Set 3

Task 1: Short Passage with Questions (Vacation Time)

Core Writing Skills Practice
Core skill: Write narratives to develop real or imagined experiences or events using effective technique, descriptive details, and clear event sequences.
Answer: Use the Narrative Writing Rubric to review the work and give a score out of 4.

Q1. Give a score of 0, 1, or 2 based on how well the answer meets the criteria listed.
- It should explain that Max is staying home or staying in town, whereas Quinn and Hoy are going away.

Q2. Give a score of 0, 1, or 2 based on how well the answer meets the criteria listed.
- It should give a personal opinion on whether the plans sound interesting or dull.
- It should explain why the student has that opinion.
- Either opinion is acceptable as long as it is supported.

Task 2: Short Passage with Questions (The Hobbit)

Core Writing Skills Practice
Core skill: Write narratives to develop real or imagined experiences or events using effective technique, descriptive details, and clear event sequences.
Answer: Use the Narrative Writing Rubric to review the work and give a score out of 4.

Q1. Give a score of 0, 1, or 2 based on how well the answer meets the criteria listed.
- It should make a valid inference about why the grandfather gave Adam the book.
- Valid inferences could include that the grandfather knew that Adam liked fantasy books, that the grandfather thought that Adam would like the book, or that the grandfather wanted to share a book that he liked with his grandson.

Q2. Give a score of 0, 1, or 2 based on how well the answer meets the criteria listed.
- It should explain that Adam likes imagining amazing places that could never really exist.

Q3. Give a score of 0, 1, 2, 3, or 4 based on how well the answer meets the criteria listed.
- It should describe what type of books the student likes most.
- It should explain why the student likes those types of book.

Task 3: Long Passage with Essay Question

Use the Informative/Explanatory Writing Rubric to review the work and give a score out of 4.

Task 4: Personal Narrative Writing Task

Use the Narrative Writing Rubric to review the work and give a score out of 4.

Practice Set 4

Task 1: Short Passage with Questions (Not So Simple)

Core Writing Skills Practice
Core skill: Draw evidence from literary texts to support analysis, reflection, and research.
Answer: The student should relate the illustration to how the donkey feels at the end of the passage. The answer may refer to how the donkey feels upset, confused, or disappointed.

Q1. Give a score of 0, 1, or 2 based on how well the answer meets the criteria listed.
- It should summarize the main events in the passage.
- The summary should include that the donkey wanted to sound like the grasshopper, starting eating dew like the grasshopper, but still could not sing.

Q2. Give a score of 0, 1, or 2 based on how well the answer meets the criteria listed.
- It should explain that the main theme is about things not being as simple as you think.
- It may describe how eating what the grasshopper ate could not make the donkey sound like a grasshopper.

Task 2: Short Passage with Questions (The Deepest of Deeps)

Core Writing Skills Practice
Core skill: Demonstrate command of the conventions of standard English grammar and usage when writing or speaking.
Answer: The student should list three words with the suffix -est and include their meanings. For example, the student could list coldest/the most cold, roughest/the most rough, and shyest/the most shy.

Q1. Give a score of 0, 1, or 2 based on how well the answer meets the criteria listed.
- It should explain that the information about Mount Everest is used to show how deep the Mariana Trench is.
- It may explain that the Mariana Trench is deeper than Mount Everest is tall.

Q2. Give a score of 0, 1, or 2 based on how well the answer meets the criteria listed.
- It should explain that the trench formed when two plates met and one plate moved under the other one.

Task 3: Opinion Piece Writing Task

Use the Opinion Writing Rubric to review the work and give a score out of 4.

Task 4: Short Story Writing Task

Use the Narrative Writing Rubric to review the work and give a score out of 4.

Practice Set 5

Task 1: Short Passage with Questions (To the Moon)

Core Writing Skills Practice

Core skill: Determine the meaning of general academic and domain-specific words or phrases in a text relevant to a grade 4 topic or subject area.

Answer: The student should explain that the word *colonize* means "to settle in an area" or "to make a settlement." The student may base the meaning on the word *colony* and the suffix *-ize* or the use of the word in the passage.

Q1. Give a score of 0, 1, or 2 based on how well the answer meets the criteria listed.
- It should identify that the main purpose is to explain that NASA's Apollo 11 mission was not the first time an object had been on the Moon.

Q2. Give a score of 0, 1, or 2 based on how well the answer meets the criteria listed.
- It should identify a detail that the student found interesting or surprising.
- It should include a brief explanation of why the detail is interesting or surprising.

Task 2: Short Passage with Questions (Rex the Superhero)

Core Writing Skills Practice

Core skill: Write narratives to develop real or imagined experiences or events using effective technique, descriptive details, and clear event sequences.

Answer: The student should describe what happens when Rex catches the thief from his point of view and include details about his feelings of fear.

Q1. Give a score of 0, 1, or 2 based on how many similes are identified. The similes are listed below.
- "His long red cape flowed off his back like flames dancing in the wind."
- "His legs started shaking like jelly, and he was too afraid to even shout at the thief."

Q2. Give a score of 0, 1, or 2 based on how well the answer meets the criteria listed.
- It should explain that Rex is too scared to take the purse back or shout at the thief.
- It should tell how Rex learns that he is afraid or learns that being a superhero is not easy.

Q3. Give a score of 0, 1, 2, 3, or 4 based on how well the answer meets the criteria listed.
- It should identify that Rex's main problem is that he is afraid.
- It should explain that Rex's fear makes it difficult for him to act like a superhero.

Task 3: Long Passage with Essay Question

Use the Informative/Explanatory Writing Rubric to review the work and give a score out of 4.

Task 4: Personal Narrative Writing Task

Use the Narrative Writing Rubric to review the work and give a score out of 4.

Practice Set 6

Task 1: Short Passage with Questions (The Race)

Core Writing Skills Practice

Core skill: Write narratives to develop real or imagined experiences or events using effective technique, descriptive details, and clear event sequences.

Answer: Use the Narrative Writing Rubric to review the work and give a score out of 4.

Q1. Give a score of 0, 1, or 2 based on how well the answer meets the criteria listed.
- It should explain that Sean drives very fast, whereas Ben drives slowly.
- It may describe Sean's driving as dangerous and Ben's driving as safe.

Q2. Give a score of 0, 1, or 2 based on how many words are identified and described.
- The words identified could include "roared," "thunder," "leapt," and "flew."
- It should identify that the words create an image of speed.

Task 2: Short Passage with Questions (Come Sail Away)

Core Writing Skills Practice

Core skill: Draw evidence from literary texts to support analysis, reflection, and research.

Answer: The student should give two examples of how the day would be different. The student may describe how Steven would feel happier, how Steven would be enjoying sharing the day, or how Steven and his son would be sailing the boat together.

Q1. Give a score of 0, 1, or 2 based on how well the answer meets the criteria listed.
- It should infer that Steven feels sad about sailing on his own.
- It may explain that Steven wishes that his children were with him.

Q2. Give a score of 0, 1, or 2 based on how well the answer meets the criteria listed.
- It should state whether going sailing would be exciting or relaxing.
- It should explain why the student has that opinion.
- Either opinion is acceptable as long as it is supported.

Task 3: Short Story Writing Task

Use the Narrative Writing Rubric to review the work and give a score out of 4.

Task 4: Opinion Piece Writing Task

Use the Opinion Writing Rubric to review the work and give a score out of 4.

Practice Set 7

Task 1: Short Passage with Questions (Clear Blue Sky)

Core Writing Skills Practice

Core skill: Draw evidence from informational texts to support analysis, reflection, and research.

Answer: The student should identify the main purpose as being to explain why the sky is blue. The student should infer that the audience is young people based on the tone, the language used, or how information is given in a simple way.

Q1. Give a score of 0, 1, or 2 based on how well the answer meets the criteria listed.
- It should explain that red and orange have the longest wavelengths, that yellow and green have medium wavelengths, and that blue has the shortest wavelength.

Q2. Give a score of 0, 1, or 2 based on how well the answer meets the criteria listed.
- It should explain that the sky appears blue because of the way that light is scattered.

Task 2: Short Passage with Questions (Harm's Diary)

Core Writing Skills Practice

Core skill: Conduct short research projects that build knowledge through investigation of different aspects of a topic.

Answer: The student should list the following presidents and years: John Adams (1797); Thomas Jefferson (1801), James Madison (1809), James Monroe (1817), John Quincy Adams (1825), Andrew Jackson (1829), Martin Van Buren (1837), William Henry Harrison (1841), and John Tyler (1845).

Q1. Give a score of 0, 1, or 2 based on how well the answer meets the criteria listed.
- It should explain that Harmanie is referring to how she will learn new information.

Q2. Give a score of 0, 1, or 2 based on how well the answer meets the criteria listed.
- It should give two valid details that show that Harmanie is a curious person.
- The details given could include that she decides to read an encyclopedia, that she says that she is fascinated by encyclopedias, that she reads about a range of different things, or that she says she learned a lot and wants to learn more.

Task 3: Long Passage with Essay Question

Use the Narrative Writing Rubric to review the work and give a score out of 4.

Task 4: Explanatory Writing Task

Use the Informative/Explanatory Writing Rubric to review the work and give a score out of 4.

Practice Set 8

Task 1: Short Passage with Questions (Volcanoes)

Core Writing Skills Practice

Core skill: Write informative/explanatory texts to examine a topic and convey ideas and information clearly.
Answer: Use the Informative/Explanatory Writing Rubric to give a score out of 4.

Q1. Give a score of 0, 1, or 2 based on how many terms are correctly defined.
- It should define magma as melted rock below the earth's surface.
- It should define lava as melted rock above the earth's surface.

Q2. Give a score of 0, 1, or 2 based on how well the answer meets the criteria listed.
- It should explain that the author describes how lava would melt a steel rod in seconds to show how hot lava is.

Task 2: Short Passage with Questions (Dangerous Dreams)

Core Writing Skills Practice

Core skill: Draw evidence from literary texts to support analysis, reflection, and research.
Answer: The student should give a reasonable description of Filbert's feelings and explain them. The answer may refer to how he feels upset, annoyed, or impatient.

Q1. Give a score of 0, 1, or 2 based on how well the answer meets the criteria listed.
- The details given could include that the main character is an elf and that the passage is about hunting dragons.

Q2. Give a score of 0, 1, or 2 based on how well the answer meets the criteria listed.
- It should give a reasonable inference about how Filbert's father feels and support the inference with details from the passage.
- A reasonable inference could be that Filbert's father feels like Filbert's plans are not practical, are too much, or are silly.

Q3. Give a score of 0, 1, 2, 3, or 4 based on how well the answer meets the criteria listed.
- It should describe a time when the student was told he or she was too young to do something. It should include details about how the student felt.

Task 3: Opinion Piece Writing Task

Use the Opinion Writing Rubric to review the work and give a score out of 4.

Task 4: Short Story Writing Task

Use the Narrative Writing Rubric to review the work and give a score out of 4.

Practice Set 9

Task 1: Short Passage with Questions (Easy Ice Cream)

Core Writing Skills Practice
Core skill: Draw evidence from informational texts to support analysis, reflection, and research.
Answer: The student should identify that the passage is organized in order or in sequence from first to last, and tell how this suits its purpose of telling how to complete a task.

Q1. Give a score of 0, 1, or 2 based on how well the answer meets the criteria listed.
- It should explain that the main purpose of the passage is to instruct or to teach readers how to do something.

Q2. Give a score of 0, 1, or 2 based on how well the answer meets the criteria listed.
- It should give an opinion on whether the student thinks that the ice cream would be easy to make.
- It should use details from the passage to support the opinion.

Task 2: Short Passage with Questions (Going on a Picnic)

Core Writing Skills Practice
Core skill: Write opinion pieces on topics or texts, supporting a point of view with reasons and information.
Answer: The student should describe benefits and drawbacks of doing things on your own. The answer may be based on personal opinion or experiences, or could also refer to the passage.

Q1. Give a score of 0, 1, or 2 based on how many activities are correctly listed.
- The activities listed could include any of the following: eats sandwiches, watches the birds, watches people, reads a book, sits by herself.

Q2. Give a score of 0, 1, or 2 based on how well the answer meets the criteria listed.
- It should circle the word relaxing.
- It should use details to shows that the narrator's time in the park is relaxing.

Task 3: Long Passage with Essay Question

Use the Informative/Explanatory Writing Rubric to review the work and give a score out of 4.

Task 4: Explanatory Writing Task

Use the Informative/Explanatory Writing Rubric to review the work and give a score out of 4.

Practice Set 10

Task 1: Short Passage with Questions (Submarines)

Core Writing Skills Practice

Core skill: Draw evidence from informational texts to support analysis, reflection, and research.
Answer: The student should give an example of a good name for a submarine and explain the choice. The name may refer to its features, appearance, or actions.

Q1. Give a score of 0, 1, or 2 based on how well the answer meets the criteria listed.
- It should explain that submarines needed to resurface to charge their batteries.
- It may explain that submarines operated on battery power while they were submerged.

Q2. Give a score of 0, 1, or 2 based on how many ways are described.
- The differences described could include that submarines are no longer powered by diesel engines, are now powered by nuclear engines, or no longer need to surface to recharge.

Task 2: Short Passage with Questions (The Wolf)

Core Writing Skills Practice

Core skill: Conduct short research projects that build knowledge through investigation of different aspects of a topic.
Answer: The student should list three tips for keeping safe from wolves, such as never feeding wolves, keeping garbage sealed, or feeding pet animals inside.

Q1. Give a score of 0, 1, or 2 based on how well the answer meets the criteria listed.
- It should explain that people took over the wolves' land and that people culled wolves.

Q2. Give a score of 0, 1, or 2 based on how well the answer meets the criteria listed.
- It should make a reasonable prediction about wolf numbers and support the opinion.
- A valid prediction could be that wolf numbers will increase because they are now protected, or that wolf numbers will decrease because people probably still want to live on the wolves' land.

Q3. Give a score of 0, 1, 2, 3, or 4 based on how well the answer meets the criteria listed.
- It should state an opinion on whether or not it is important to protect animal species.
- It should use information from the passage to support the opinion, and may also use prior knowledge and personal experience.

Task 3: Short Story Writing Task

Use the Narrative Writing Rubric to review the work and give a score out of 4.

Task 4: Opinion Piece Writing Task

Use the Opinion Writing Rubric to review the work and give a score out of 4.

INFORMATIVE/EXPLANATORY WRITING RUBRIC

This writing rubric is based on the Common Core standards and describes the features that are expected in student writing. Give students a score out of 4 based on how well the answer meets the criteria. Then average the scores to give a total score out of 4. Students can also be given feedback and guidance based on the criteria below.

	Score	Notes
Organization and Purpose To receive a full score, the response will: • have an opening that introduces the topic • have a clear focus • be well-organized with related information grouped together • include formatting such as headings when appropriate • provide a concluding statement or section		
Evidence and Elaboration To receive a full score, the response will: • develop the topic with facts, details, quotations, or examples • include relevant text-based evidence when appropriate		
Written Expression To receive a full score, the response will: • be clear and easy to understand • have good transitions between ideas • use language to communicate ideas effectively		
Writing Conventions To receive a full score, the response will: • have few or no spelling errors • have few or no grammar errors • have few or no capitalization errors • have few or no punctuation errors		
Total Score		

OPINION WRITING RUBRIC

This writing rubric is based on the Common Core standards and describes the features that are expected in student writing. Give students a score out of 4 based on how well the answer meets the criteria. Then average the scores to give a total score out of 4. Students can also be given feedback and guidance based on the criteria below.

	Score	Notes
Organization and Purpose To receive a full score, the response will: • have an opening that introduces the topic and states an opinion • have a clear focus • be well-organized with related information grouped together • provide a concluding statement or section		
Evidence and Elaboration To receive a full score, the response will: • provide reasons to support the opinion • develop the topic with facts, details, or examples • include relevant text-based evidence when appropriate		
Written Expression To receive a full score, the response will: • be clear and easy to understand • have good transitions between ideas • use language to communicate ideas effectively		
Writing Conventions To receive a full score, the response will: • have few or no spelling errors • have few or no grammar errors • have few or no capitalization errors • have few or no punctuation errors		
Total Score		

NARRATIVE WRITING RUBRIC

This writing rubric is based on the Common Core standards and describes the features that are expected in student writing. Give students a score out of 4 based on how well the answer meets the criteria. Then average the scores to give a total score out of 4. Students can also be given feedback and guidance based on the criteria below.

	Score	Notes
Organization and Purpose To receive a full score, the response will: • have an effective opening that introduces the situation, characters, or event • have a logical and organized event sequence • have an effective ending		
Development and Elaboration To receive a full score, the response will: • have clearly developed characters, setting, and events • use dialogue and descriptions effectively • use concrete words and sensory details • use narrative techniques effectively • have an appropriate style		
Written Expression To receive a full score, the response will: • be clear and easy to understand • have good transitions between ideas • use language to communicate ideas effectively		
Writing Conventions To receive a full score, the response will: • have few or no spelling errors • have few or no grammar errors • have few or no capitalization errors • have few or no punctuation errors		
Total Score		

Made in the USA
Middletown, DE
14 February 2017